Healing

By Yolonda F. Marzest
Illustrations by Justina Framstad

Copyright © 2012, 2014 Yolonda F. Marzest.

All rights reserved. No part of this book may be used or reproduced by any means, graphic, electronic, or mechanical, including photocopying, recording, taping or by any information storage retrieval system without the written permission of the publisher except in the case of brief quotations embodied in critical articles and reviews.

Interior graphics by Justina Framstad.

WestBow Press books may be ordered through booksellers or by contacting:

WestBow Press
A Division of Thomas Nelson & Zondervan
1663 Liberty Drive
Bloomington, IN 47403
www.westbowpress.com
1 (866) 928-1240

Because of the dynamic nature of the Internet, any web addresses or links contained in this book may have changed since publication and may no longer be valid. The views expressed in this work are solely those of the author and do not necessarily reflect the views of the publisher, and the publisher hereby disclaims any responsibility for them.

Any people depicted in stock imagery provided by Thinkstock are models, and such images are being used for illustrative purposes only.
Certain stock imagery © Thinkstock.

ISBN: 978-1-4908-2497-0 (sc)
ISBN: 978-1-4908-2498-7 (e)

Library of Congress Control Number: 2014902135

Scriptures taken from the Holy Bible, New International Version®, NIV®. Copyright © 1973, 1978, 1984, 2011 by Biblica, Inc.™ Used by permission of Zondervan. All rights reserved worldwide. www.zondervan.com The "NIV" and "New International Version" are trademarks registered in the United States Patent and Trademark Office by Biblica, Inc.™ All rights reserved.

Scripture quotations taken from the Holy Bible, New Living Translation, copyright 1996, 2004. Used by permission of Tyndale House Publishers, Inc., Wheaton, Illinois 60189. All rights reserved.

Printed in the United States of America.

WestBow Press rev. date: 02/12/2014

Dedication

This little book is dedicated to all women who have opened their hearts to love
To women who have been hurt and found no answers to their hurt
To women who need a Word and answers
To women who want to love again and can love again

Acknowledgements

First and foremost I have to thank God for bringing this lovely book out of me and all it has to bring for those who are allowing these words to change their lives.

To my beautiful daughter Brittney, who has been a consistent non failing support to her mother and believing I can achieve the completion of this book. Thank you, Brittney for believing. Always to my family, thank you, you have given me the gift to move on and grow in-spite of…

Thank you to those who have encouraged me to put this work out to the public and all the encouragement that has been consistent over the years Theresa Johnson, Priscilla Gale-Black, Cora Phillips and Patricia Hairston.

My cousin Gloria Darby, for setting up my first reading and support through getting this project completed. I cannot express my appreciation enough, I say thank you! To all the ladies who participated in my first book reading, Christine Espinoza, Shelly Trinidad and of course Lisa Leslie-Lockwood who opened her beautiful home to experience the review of the book, thank you all very much.

Michelle Anderson-Day, thanks my friend for introducing me to my first writers group and all the encouragement in the early days of writing.

Thank you Justina Framstad, for working with me over the years to seeing this book into reality. Thank you for the beautiful art work you allowed me to purchase from you to include in this work and the tireless work you added to make this book to be a great success.

Finally thanks to all who have supported me whether it be by conversations, gentle words, prayers or quietly. And of course to the readers, a big Thank You all for purchasing and supporting this work.

You don't deserve pain,
You deserve the love of God,
you don't deserve infidelity

"Loyalty makes a person attractive. It is better to be poor than dishonest."
(Proverbs 19:22 New Living Translation)

You deserve the Best God Has to offer,
you don't deserve a fake or fraud

"For God so loved the world that He gave His One and only Son..." (John 3:16 New International Version)

You deserve the real mate from God,
you don't deserve hate & jealousy

"You must not covet your neighbor's house. You must not covet your neighbor's wife, male or female servant, ox, donkey, or anything else that belongs to your neighbor." (Exodus 20:17 New Living Translation)

You deserve Love from God,
you don't deserve the pain from another

"How delightful is your love, my sister, my bride! How much more pleasing is your love than wine, and the fragrance of your perfume than any spice!" (Song of Songs 4:10 New International Version)

You deserve lifes happiness from another,
*you don't deserve anyone else's pain,
from their past failures and faults*

"This is my commandment: Love each other the same way I have loved you. There is no greater love than to lay down one's life for one's friends." (John 15: 12 - 13 New Living Translation)

You deserve the love of other's from their happiness
and successes,
God has shown them
you don't deserve anyone else's pain

"Live happily with the woman you love through all the meaningless days of life that God has given you under the sun. The wife God gives you is your reward for all your earthly toil." (Ecclesiastes 9:9 New Living Translation)

You deserve God to support you through your own pain

"Oh, that I might have my request, that God would grant my desire." "At least I can take comfort in this: Despite the pain, I have not denied the Words of the Holy One." (Job 6:8 & 10 New Living Translation)

You deserve the love of a real man
sent from God,
*satan always sends counterfeit
dressed in God's clothes*

"without love, unforgiving, slanderous, without self-control, brutal, not lovers of good," "They are the kind who worm their way into homes and gain control over weak-willed women, who are loaded down with sins and are swayed by all kinds of evil desires." (2Timothy 3:3 & 6 New International Version)

Remember to just Trust in God and
He will send the real deal!

"Trust in the Lord with all your heart and lean not to your own understanding: in all your ways acknowledge Him, and He will make your paths straight." (Proverbs 3:5 New International Version)

God heals hurt, pain and anger,
God will send joy in the morning and the man
of your life will be Beautiful, Honorable,
Trusting, Loving and Kind to Your Heart
and most of all Love Unconditional,
he will be true to you and a friend forever!
You deserve this,
you don't deserve a man who wants to be and is not

"He heals the brokenhearted and binds up their wounds." (Psalm 147:3 New International Version)

You deserve a man who is a man,
and loves himself as he is!
Remember God is healing your heart
because God is where your Trust really is,
and He will always honor, love
and bless His children abundantly

"Her husband has full confidence in her and lacks nothing of value."
"She brings him good, not harm, all of the days of her life." "Her Husband is respected at the city gate,
where he takes his seat among the elders of the land." (Proverbs 31: 11-12 & 23 New International Version)

You opened your heart for love and God
knows this, He does not like it when
His children are taken for granted
and are mis-treated
He does not like a con list that does not balance
with a pro list! God will and is healing your
heart right now, it is just hard to feel because
you are human but you are being
Healed right Now!

"Hope deferred makes the heart sick, but a dream fulfilled is a tree of life."
(Proverbs 13:12 New Living Translation)

You do deserve the best God has to offer and God is always on time.

"There is a time for everything, and a season for every activity under heaven:"
(Ecclesiastes 3:1 New International Version)

Don't look back, look ahead
blessings are coming!
You deserve a heaven sent relationship
with a true man of God,
Don't look back, look ahead
miracles & blessings are coming fast!

"Forget the former things; do not dwell on the past. See, I am doing a new thing! Now it springs up..."
(Isaiah 43: 18-19 New International Version)

You deserve happiness,
unselfishness, fidelity, companionship,
You deserve to be a wife on a pedestal,
You deserve to be a Queen with a King,
You deserve the protection of your King,

You deserve happiness and honor all the time

Don't look back!!

"Husbands, love your wives, just as Christ loved the church and gave Himself up for her to make her holy cleansing her by the washing with water through the Word, and to present her to Himself as a radiant church, without stain or wrinkle or any other blemish, but holy and blameless. In this same way, husbands ought to love their wives as their own bodies. He who loves his wife loves himself."

(Epeshians 5:25 - 28 New International Version)

Holy Spirit Guided

Look ahead Miracles & Blessings
are coming fast!
You deserve 100% of what God has for you
You deserve peace and happiness!
You deserve respect and support!
Your spirit deserves to be uplifted daily!
Don't look back Look ahead
Miracles & Blessings are coming FAST!
God will bless you today!
God is healing your heart, God is love & loves you
unconditionally
This is what you deserve!

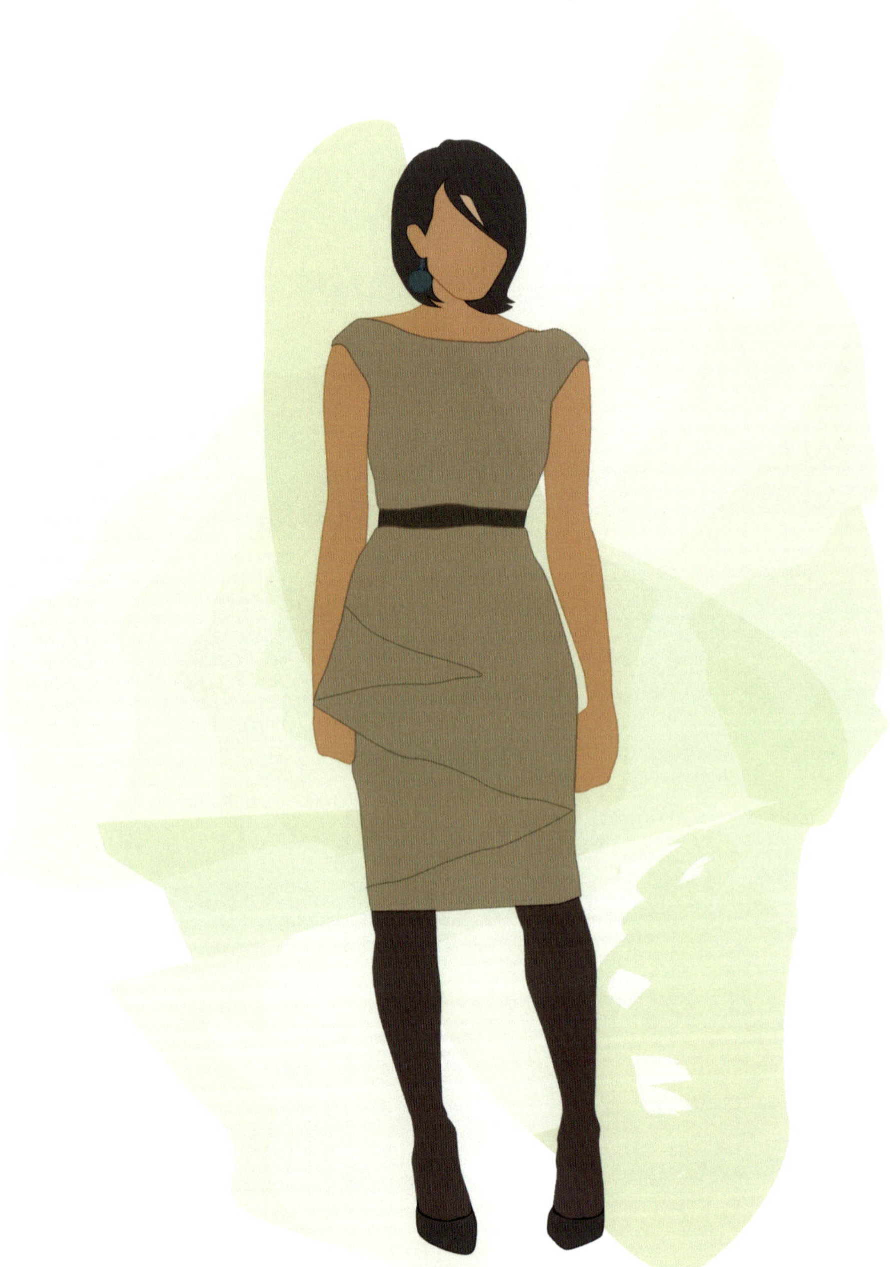

Study Guide & Questions to Ponder page 1:

Genesis 2:21-25 and Genesis 3
What is God's first covenant with man and woman?
What attempted the demise of this covenant with man and woman?
What was the result of their failure to listen to God's instruction?

Marriage Scriptures to consider:
Genesis 2:18 - 24
Genesis 24:58 - 60
Jeremiah 33:10 - 11
Malachi 2:14 - 15
Matthew 5:32
Matthew 19:6
Romans 7:2 - 3
Ephesians 5:21 - 33
Hebrews 13:4

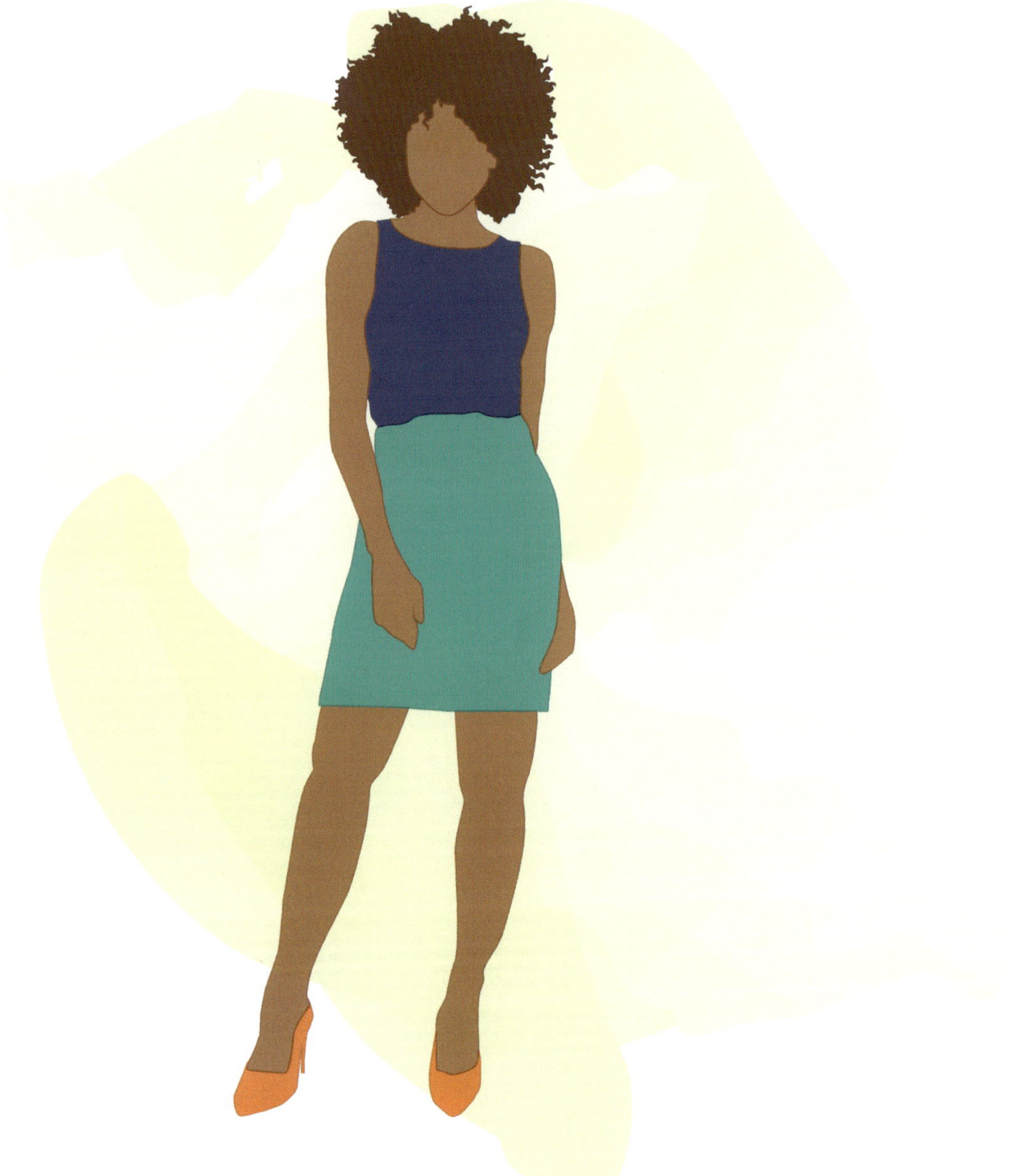

Study Guide & Questions to ponder page 2:

Proverbs 5:1 - 23, 6:20 - 35, 7:1 - 27, 12:4, 18:22, 19:14 & 31:10 - 31
What is God's warning?
What does God say about adultery?
Is there such a thing as an adulteress?
What happens when you compromise?
What should the character of a wife look like?
What (who) is a "Good Thing"?
What does prudent mean?
What does a 'Proverbs' woman reflect?

Hababkkuk 2:1 - 4
What is your vision for your life?
Have you ever thought about writing it down?

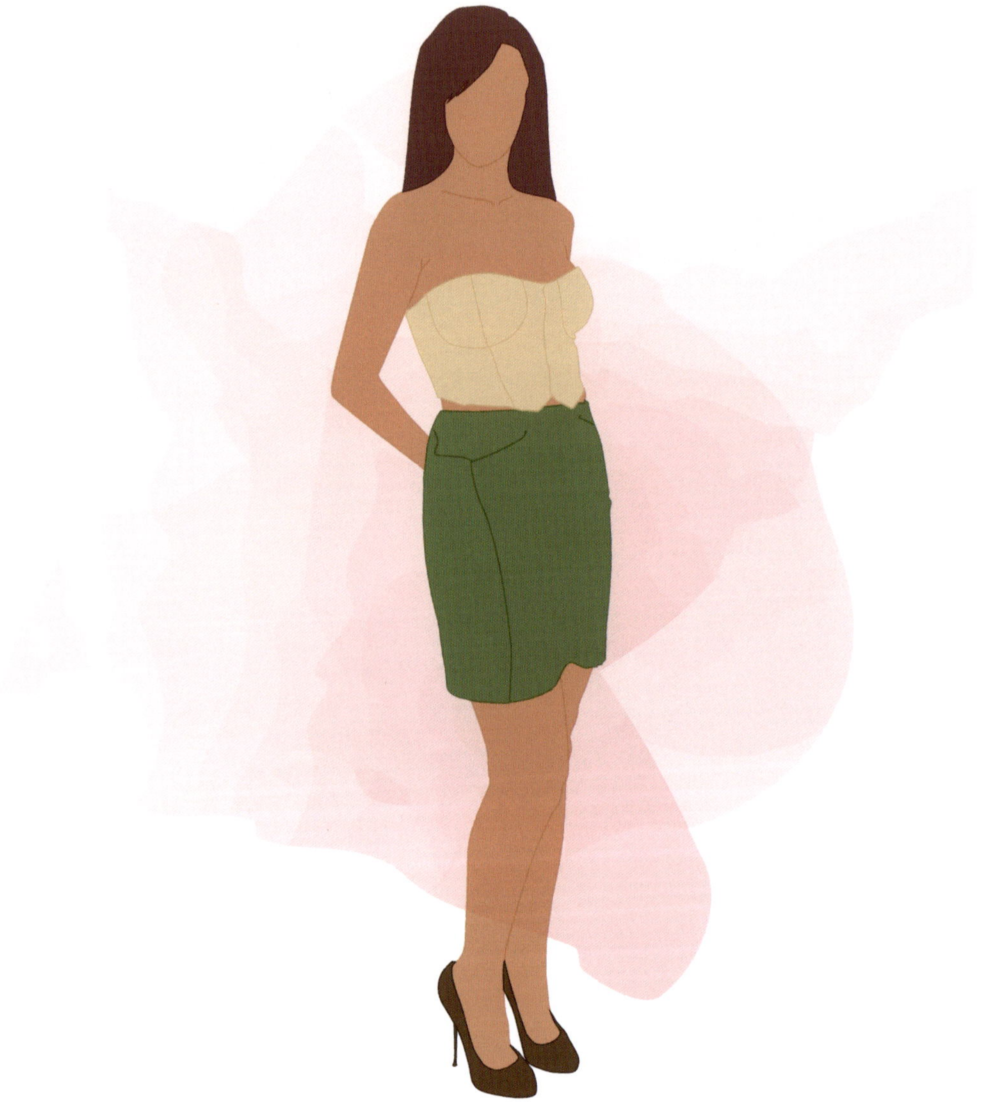

Study Guide & Questions to ponder page 3:

Luke 7:36 - 50
What did you learn about the woman's faith?

Matthew 6 & 25:1 - 13, 21
What is God's response to those who are faithful?
Can you look for God to answer your prayer request and realize your vision in the physical if you are faithful?
How do you fast and pray to hear God's answer for your hopes to be realized?
Is the Bridegroom of your life coming?
Have your prepared for the Bridegroom to come into your life?
Do you have oil in your lamp?
Will you be sleep or wide awake?

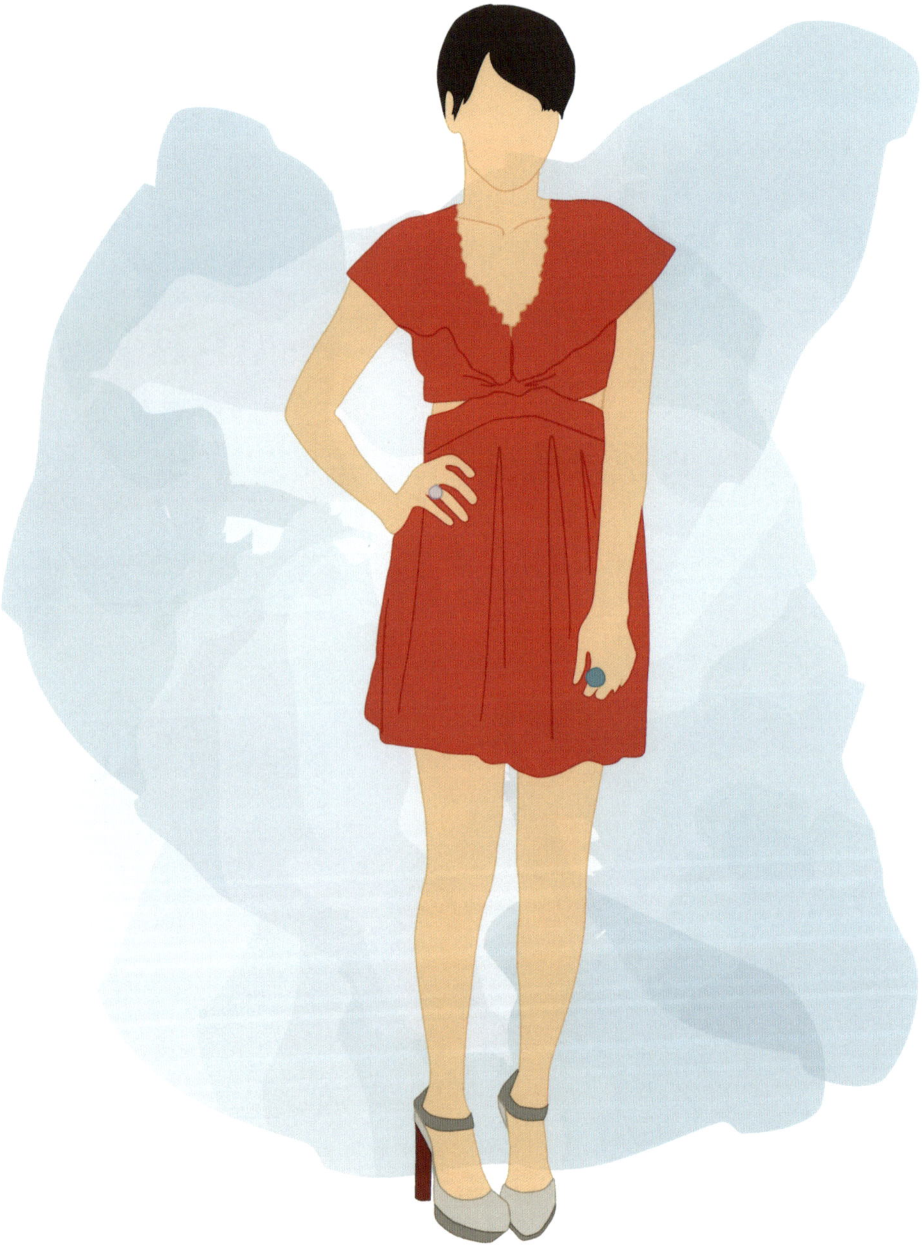

Study Guide & Questions to Ponder page 4:

Phillipians 4:6 - 7
Have you prepared your petition to God?
What are you doing while you are waiting for the answer to your petition?

Romans 12:1 - 2
What is God's will?
Can you TRUST that God's will for your partner, soul mate of your life is good?

John 3:27 - 30
What are you to do while you're waiting on the Bridegroom?

Romans 7:1 - 6
What does God say about marriage?
What does God say about divorce?
Are you, trusting God for your wedding, marriage, divorce or singleness?

1Corinthians 6:12 - 20 & 7
How are we to live sexually?
Is it good to take a gamble on your life and health to satisfy your flesh?
Is trusting God enough to meet your human needs?
Why is it good to stay single?
When should you get married?
What does it mean to burn?

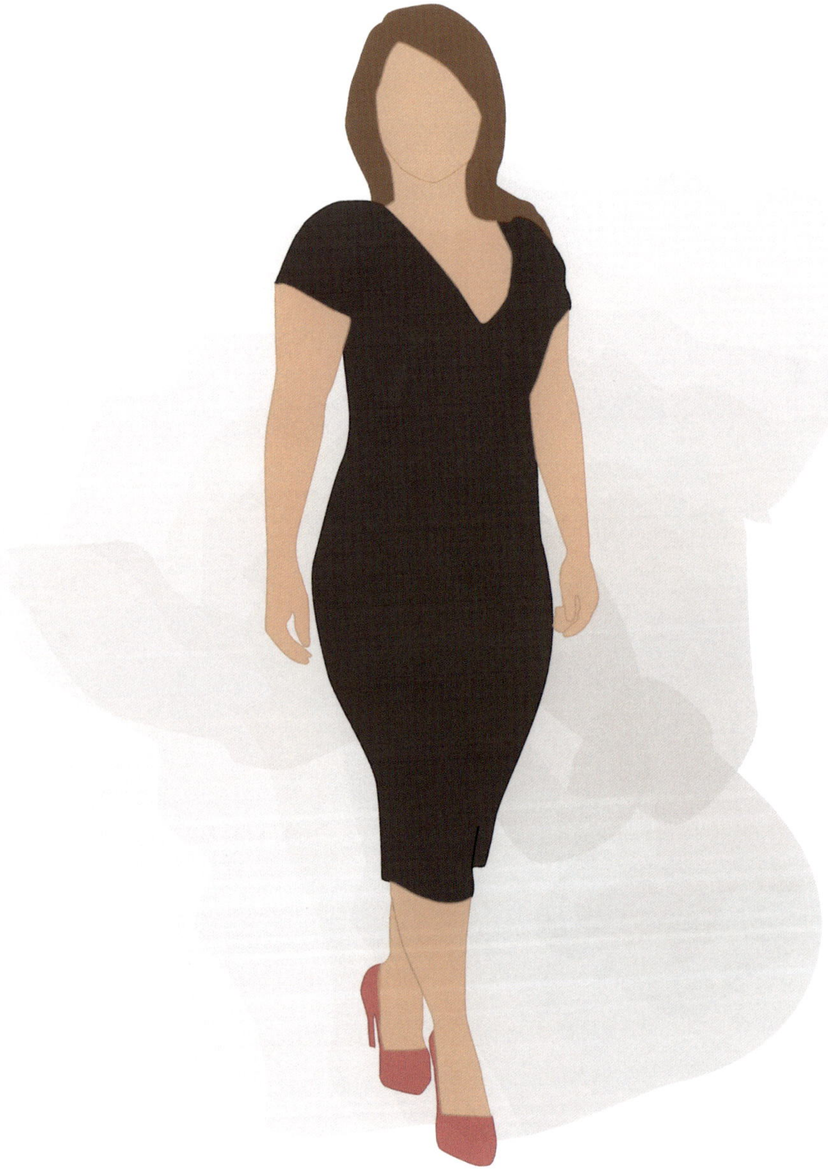

Study Guide & Questions to Ponder page 5:

Ephesians 5:22 - 33
How should a woman be loved?
Is the woman to take care of her husband like Jesus takes care of the church?
How is a man to view his wife?
What is the only command a wife is to do for her husband according to this chapter?

1 Timothy 5:7 - 9
Are you to worry about the fathers who don't take care of their children/family?
What will God do for those who walk away from their children?

2 Timothy 3:3 - 9
Based on this study guide reading God's Word & His truths how will you live your life?
What does the Word of God say about women who choose not to listen to His Word?

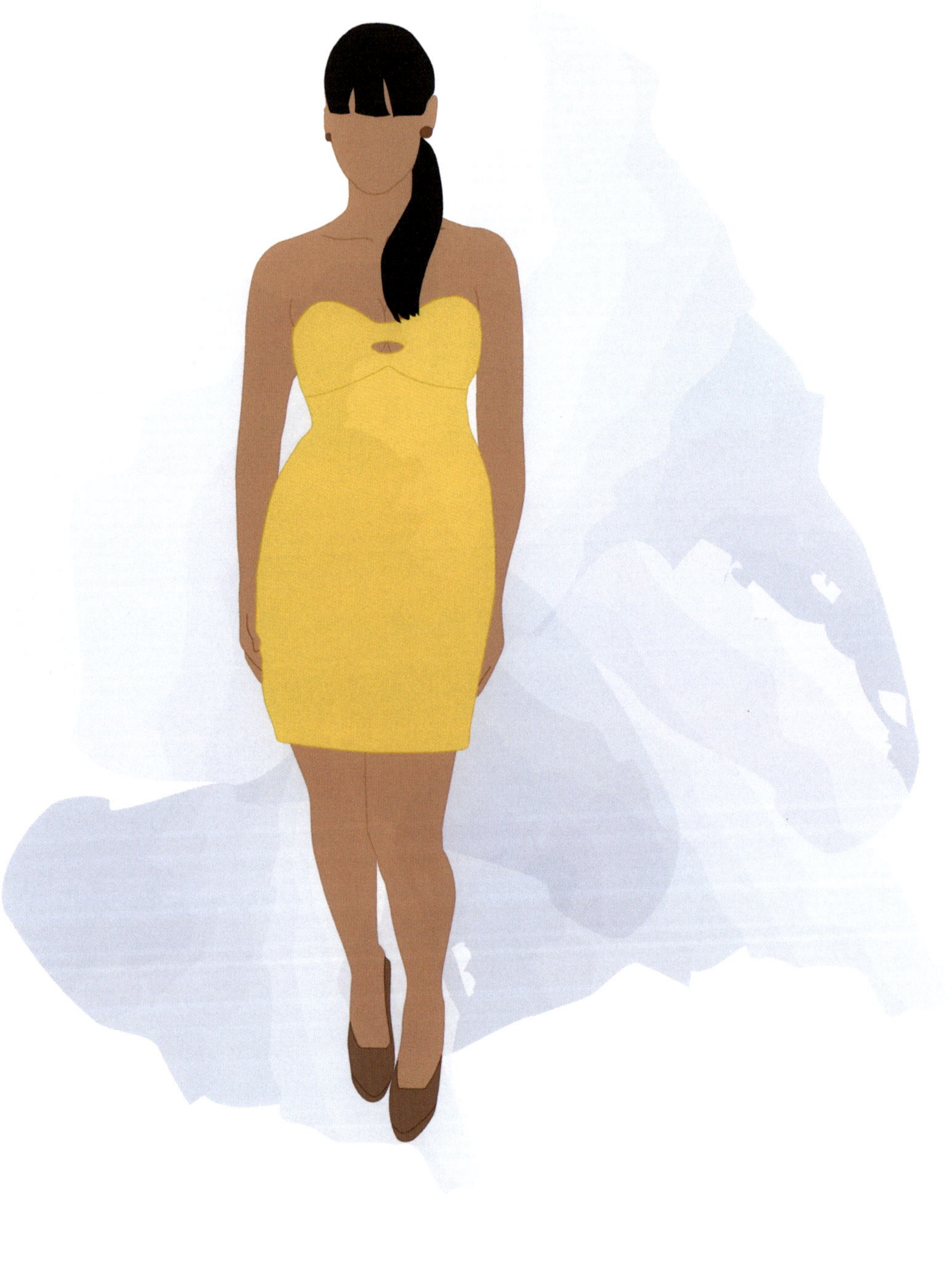

Study Guide & Questions to Ponder page 6:

Read the Song of Solomon

How is a man supposed to, according to the Word, to love, make love and cherish woman?

God is the Creator of all on this Earth and He really, really created sex and it is good when done as He created.

You can have sex and make love to the man of your dreams, that is the man God always has/had in plans for you, we just have to trust God first…

.

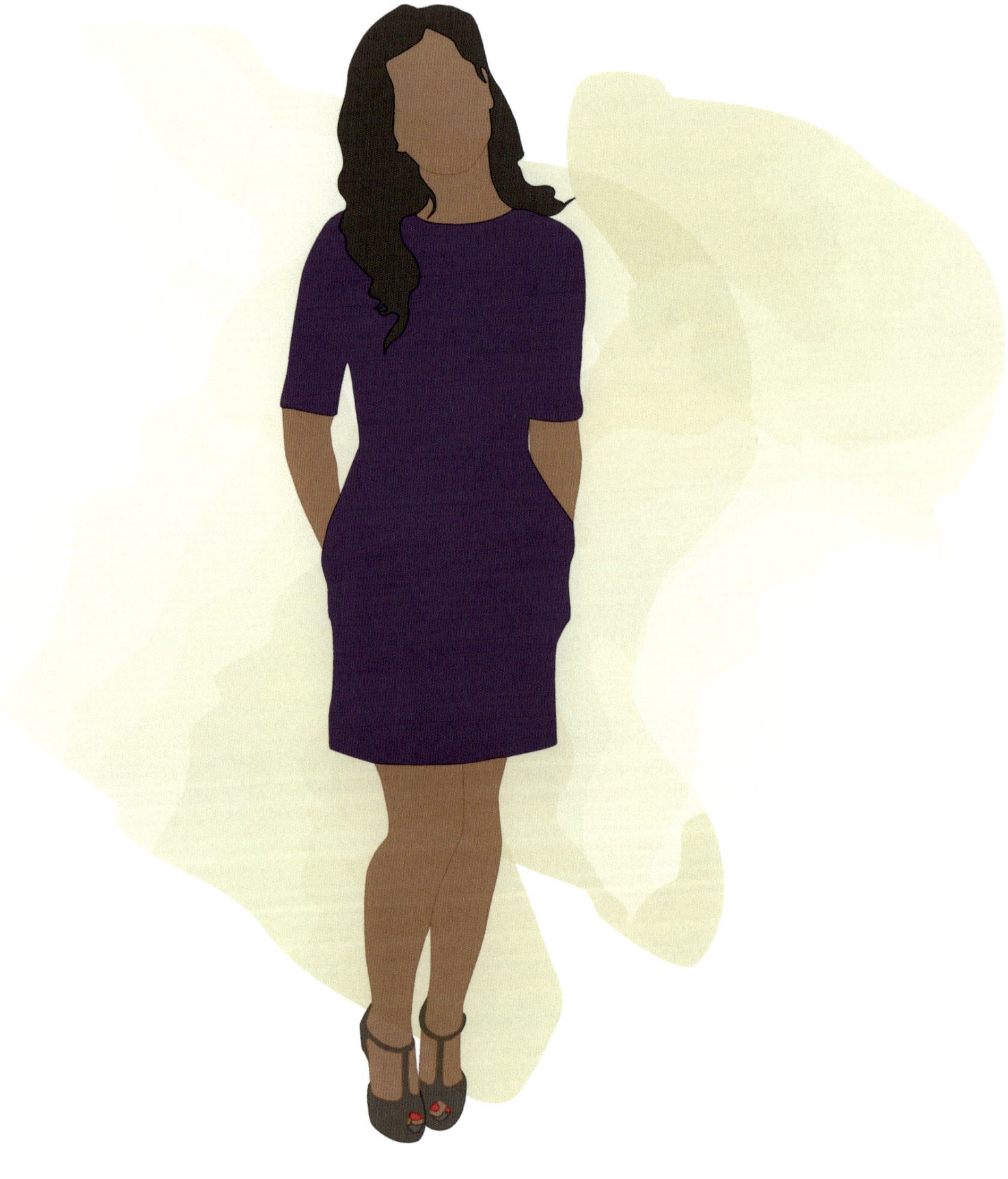

About the Author

Yolonda F. Marzest, MSW attended the University of Washington where she received her BASW and MSW. Works as a Manager of Program Operations for the Alliance for Child Welfare Excellence – University of Washington School of Social Work. Yolonda has taught Christian classes for single women titled "Why Her? Not Me." This is the first literary work that Yolonda has had the honor of writing and publishing.

About the Artist

Justina is 26 years old with the dream of becoming an illustrator. She received her Associates of Art and Associates of Fine Art from Shoreline Community College in Shoreline, WA in 2012. She was born in California and moved to Seattle when she was 4. She has been doing freelance graphic design and illustration since 2007 and is almost entirely self taught. Justina currently lives in New York, New York

CPSIA information can be obtained at www.ICGtesting.com
Printed in the USA
BVIW12n2330220315
392711BV00003B/3

9 781490 824970